MARK

Studies in This Series
Available from your Christian book store:

How to Start a Neighborhood Bible Study
A Guide to Discussion Study

Mark:
Examine the Record
(recommended as first unit of study)

Luke

The Acts of the Apostles

Romans

1 Corinthians
Challenge to Maturity

2 Corinthians and Galatians
A Call for Help and Freedom

A Study of Ephesians and Philemon

Philippians and Colossians
Letters from Prison

The Letter to the Hebrews

1 and 2 Peter
Letters to People in Trouble

The First Epistle of John and the Epistle of James

They Met Jesus
Eight Studies of New Testament Characters

Four Men of God
Abraham, Joseph, Moses, David

Psalms and Proverbs

Choose Life
Basic Doctrines of the Christian Faith

Amos
Prophet of Life-style

Conversations with Jesus Christ
from the Gospel of John

Patterns for Living with God
Twelve Old Testament Character Studies

MARK
EXAMINE THE RECORD
17 discussions for Group Bible Study

by Marilyn Kunz and Catherine Schell

TYNDALE HOUSE PUBLISHERS, INC.
Wheaton, Illinois

Sixteenth printing, July 1978
ISBN 8423-4101-3

Contents

How to Use
This Discussion Guide

Sharing leadership — why and how

Each study guide in the Neighborhood Bible Study series is prepared with the intention that the ordinary adult group will by using this guide be able to rotate the leadership of the discussion. Those who are outgoing in personality are more likely to volunteer to lead first, but within a few weeks it should be possible for almost everyone to have the privilege of directing a discussion session. Everyone, including people new to the Bible who may not yet have committed themselves to Christ, should take a turn in leading by asking the questions from the study guide.

Reasons for this approach are:

(1) The discussion leader will prepare in greater depth than the average participant.

(2) The experience of leading a study stimulates a person to be a better participant in the discussions led by others.

(3) Members of the group which changes discussion leadership weekly tend to feel that the group belongs to everyone in it. It is not "Mr. or Mrs. Smith's Bible Study."

(4) The Christian who by reason of spiritual maturity and wider knowledge of the Bible is equipped to be a spiritual leader in the group is set free to *listen* to everyone in the group in a way that is not possible when leading the discussion. He (she) takes his regular turn in leading as it comes around, but if he leads the first study in a series he must guard against the temptation to bring a great deal of outside knowledge and source material which would make others feel they could not possibly attempt to follow his example of leadership.

For study methods and discussion techniques refer to the first booklet in this series, *How to Start a Neighborhood Bible Study*, as well as to the following suggestions.

How to prepare to participate in a study using this guide

(1) Read through the designated chapter daily during the week. Use it in your daily time of meditation and prayer, asking God to teach you what he has for you in it.

(2) Take two or three of the guide questions each day and try to answer them from the passage. Use these questions as tools to dig deeper into the passage. In this way you can cover all the guide questions before the group discussion.

(3) Use the summary questions to tie together the whole chapter in your thinking.

(4) *As an alternative* to using this study in your daily quiet time, spend at least two hours in sustained study once during the week, using the above suggestions.

How to prepare to lead a study

(1) Follow the above suggestions on preparing to participate in a study. Pray for wisdom and the Holy Spirit's guidance.

(2) Familiarize yourself with the study guide questions until you can rephrase them in your own words if necessary to make you comfortable using them in the discussion.

(3) Pray for the ability to guide the discussion with love and understanding.

How to lead a study

(1) Begin with prayer for minds open to understand and hearts willing to obey the Word of the Lord. You may ask another member of the group to pray if you have asked him ahead of time.

(2) Have the Bible portion read aloud by paragraphs. Be sure to have the reading done by paragraph or thought units, *never* verse by verse. It is not necessary for everyone to read aloud, or for each to read an equal amount.

(3) Guide the group to discover what the passage says by asking the *discussion questions*. Use the suggestions from the section on "How to encourage everyone to participate."

(4) As the group discusses the Bible passage together, encourage each one to be honest in self-appraisal. You must take

the lead in spiritual honesty. Try to avoid hypocrisy in any form.

(5) Allow time at the end of the discussion to answer the *summary questions* which help to tie the whole study together.

(6) Bring the discussion to a close at the end of the time allotted. Ask one of the group members to read the *conclusion* section. Close in a prayer relevant to what has been discussed.

How to encourage everyone to participate

(1) Encourage discussion by asking several people to contribute answers to a question. "What do the rest of you think?" or "Is there anything else which could be added?" are ways of encouraging discussion.

(2) Be flexible and skip any questions which do not fit into the discussion as it progresses.

(3) Deal with irrelevant issues by suggesting that the purpose of your study is to discover what is *in the passage*. Suggest an informal chat about tangential or controversial issues after the regular study is dismissed.

(4) Receive all contributions warmly. Never bluntly reject what anyone says, even if you think the answer is incorrect. Instead ask in a friendly manner, "Where did you find that?" or "Is that actually what it says?" or "What do some of the rest of you think?" Allow the group to handle problems together.

(5) Be sure you don't talk too much as the leader. Redirect those questions which are asked you. A discussion should move in the form of an asterisk, back and forth between members, not in the form of a fan, with the discussion always coming back to the leader. The leader is to act as moderator. As members of a group get to know each other better, the discussion will move more freely, progressing from the fan to the asterisk pattern.

(6) Don't be afraid of pauses or long silences. People need time to think about the questions and the passage. Never, *never* answer your own question — either use an alternate question or move on to another area for discussion.

(7) Watch hesitant members for an indication by facial expression or body posture that they have something to say, and then give them an encouraging nod or speak their names.

(8) Discourage too talkative members from monopolizing the discussion by specifically directing questions to others. If

necessary speak privately to the over-talkative one about the need for discussion rather than lecture in the group, and enlist his aid in encouraging all to participate.

What rules make for an effective discussion?

(1) Everyone in the group should *read the Bible passage* and, if possible, use the study guide in thoughtful *study* of the passage *before* coming to the group meeting.

(2) *Stick to the Bible passage under discussion.* Discover all that you can from this section of Mark's Gospel without moving around to other books of the Bible in cross-references. This means that the person new to the Bible will not be needlessly confused, and you will avoid the danger of taking portions out of context.

(3) As your group proceeds through the Gospel of Mark, you will *build a common frame of reference.* Within a few weeks it will be possible for people to refer back to several chapters of Mark and to trace lines of thought through large sections of his Gospel.

(4) *Avoid tangents.* Many different ideas will be brought to mind as you study each chapter of Mark. If an idea is not dealt with in any detail in a particular chapter, do not let it occupy long discussion that week. Appoint a recorder in your group to make note of this and other such questions that arise from week to week. As your group studies on in the book of Mark, you will find some of these questions are answered in later chapters.

(5) Since the three-fold purpose of an inductive Bible study is to discover what the Bible portion says, what it means, and what it means to you, your group should remember that *the Gospel of Mark is the authority for your study.* The aim of your group should be to discover what Mark is saying, to discover Mark's message.

If you don't like something that Mark says, be honest enough to admit that you don't like it. Do not re-write the Bible to make it agree with your ideas. You may say that you do not agree with Mark, or that you wish he had not said this, but don't try to make him say what he does not say. It is Mark's account that you are investigating. Let him state his own case.

(6) *Apply to your own life what you discover in the study of Mark's Gospel.* Much of the vitality of any group Bible discussion depends upon honest sharing on the part of different members of the group. Discoveries made in Bible study should become guides for right action in present day life situations.

Jesus is presented ever more clearly as Mark moves through his account, so that you have the opportunity to see the evidence Mark considered certain proof that Jesus is the Messiah, the Son of God. You have the opportunity to face the implications for your life of Jesus' claims.

(7) *Let honesty with love be the attitude of your group toward one another.* Those who do not believe that Jesus is the Christ should be able to voice their doubts and questions without feeling rejected or feeling that they should cover up their true feelings. Those who do believe and are committed to Jesus as Lord and Savior should be free to share how this belief affects their lives (as appropriate to the section of Mark under discussion). Rather than trying to convince one another of your beliefs or disbeliefs, you should let yourself be searched and judged by the Gospel of Mark. You should examine the record for yourself.

Introduction to
The Gospel of Mark

Would you like to have heard the Apostle Peter tell about his experiences with Jesus? Read the Gospel according to Mark! Written about 65 A.D., Mark's Gospel is the earliest record we have of the life of Jesus. It contains Peter's eyewitness account as Mark recorded it from Peter's preaching and teaching.

We know about the author, John Mark, from brief mentions in the book of Acts, the letters of Paul and Peter, and from what is probably a personal signature in Mark 14:51, 52. Mark accompanied his relative Barnabas and the Apostle Paul on the first missionary journey but deserted the trip before it was completed. Although Paul refused to take Mark on his second journey, he did speak highly of him (in II Timothy 4:11) indicating Mark's stature as a Christian leader in later years. Peter called him "my son Mark," (I Peter 5:13). It was the house of Mark's mother Mary which was the headquarters for the Christians in Jerusalem.

The Gospel of Mark is the shortest of the four records of the life of Jesus and is characterized by vivid realism in its presentation of Jesus as fully divine and fully human. Mark devoted six out of 16 chapters to a description of the last week in Jesus' life, indicating the importance he put on these particular events. This Gospel was aimed for the Gentile Roman mind to present Jesus as the Christ, the Son of God. It was written with the expectation that a careful examination of the record would bring a definite response to the facts presented. William Barclay comments that Mark's Gospel could be called the most important book in the world.

All the available reliable manuscripts conclude at Mark 16:8, which obviously is not the conclusion of Mark's narrative. The most likely explanation is that the last part of the scroll was torn off and lost at a time when only one copy of the book existed. In our study series we shall use Luke chapter 24 as the concluding study in the life of Jesus.

DISCUSSION 1—MARK 1

Early Ministry

The first verse may be considered the author's own title to the whole book, a statement of the thesis which he sets out to prove, the good news that Jesus is the Messiah, the Son of God. "Christ" is a title, the Greek word for Messiah, meaning "anointed." Watch for the appearance of the word "Christ" again in Mark's Gospel.

In this chapter both the ministry of John the Baptist and the early ministry of Jesus are described.

Mark 1:1-8

(1) What does the quotation in verses 2, 3 tell about the messenger, his task, where he will work, and his message?

(2) In what ways does John the baptizer fulfill the Old Testament prophecy about the messenger?

(3) Describe John and his ministry. In verses 4, 7, 8 what does he preach? (To the Jews John's dress signified he was a prophet like the Old Testament prophet Elijah. His food was that of the poor.)

(4) In what ways would John's ministry prepare the people for Messiah? How does repentance prepare us to receive a Savior? What differences does John point out between himself and the one to come?

Mark 1:9-15

(5) When does Jesus appear on the scene? Locate Nazareth, Jerusalem, and the Jordan river on your map. How far does Jesus travel to be baptized by John?

(6) What are the three unique events at the baptism of Jesus? What do they indicate? How is the Trinity represented here?

(7) If you were asked to paint a mural of verses 12, 13, what kingdoms or realms would be represented? What facts regarding the temptation does Mark emphasize?

(8) What does verse 14 suggest about the outcome of Jesus' temptation? Where does Jesus begin his ministry? Compare his preaching in verse 15 with John's preaching in verses 4, 7, 8. What similarities and what differences do you see?

Mark 1:16-20

(9) From what class of society does Jesus call his first disciples? Why, do you think, does he not call some of the scribes or priests instead?

(10) Locate the sea of Galilee. What are Simon and Andrew doing? What are they called to do? What indications are there that James and John are perhaps younger and financially better off than Simon and Andrew? What reactions or comments may there have been when these four followed Jesus? What reactions would there be today?

Mark 1:21-28

(11) Locate Capernaum. What happens here? How does Jesus' teaching differ from what the people are accustomed to?

(12) How does the unclean spirit address and identify Jesus? What pronoun does the spirit use in referring to himself? What does he fear?

(13) How does verse 25 make it clear that Jesus regards the unclean spirit as a separate entity from the man it is possessing? What two commands does Jesus give? With what result? How do the people react? What surprises them?

(Do not spend a lot of time at this point discussing evil spirits. Mark will mention them a number of times in his book and you will learn more as you study further.)

Mark 1:29-34

(14) What crisis arises after the synagogue service? (It is probably mealtime.) How do the disciples react? How do you know that the woman's recovery was not just a matter of the fever breaking?

(15) What events of the day stimulate the crowd's activity at sundown? Why do they wait until sundown? (What day is it—see verse 21?)

What verbs are used to describe Jesus' treatment of disease and of demons? Why does Jesus silence the demons again as in verse 25? Why would he not desire publicity from this source?

Mark 1:35-39

(16) Think back over the events of the Sabbath (verses 21-34). In verse 35 when, where and why does Jesus pray? With what temptation is he now faced? Why do the people seek him?

(17) In his ministry of preaching and healing, upon which does Jesus place priority? Why? Where does he now go? Where does he preach in his early ministry?

Mark 1:40-45

(18) Lest the reader conclude from verse 38 that Jesus is without concern for men's physical needs, what incident does Mark relate? What question does the leper have? Why does Jesus touch him?

(19) What strict order does Jesus give the leper?

(Note—The term *leprosy* included some other skin diseases as well as leprosy itself. Under Jewish law anyone who recovered from such a skin disease had to be examined by a priest and go through a ceremony of restoration. See Leviticus 14. After receiving a certificate that he was clean, he could return to live in society.)

(20) Why, do you think, does the leper disobey? What happens when he does?

SUMMARY

(1) How does Mark begin to prove his thesis that Jesus is Messiah, the Son of God?

(2) What indications are there that Jesus is also truly human?

(3) What impressions do you get of Jesus thus far?

CONCLUSION

Mark begins his record of the life of Jesus Christ at the point of Jesus' public ministry rather than with the events of his birth as do Matthew and Luke. Mark, however, does link the coming of Jesus to the Old Testament prophecies of Messiah by pointing out the meaning and effect of John the baptizer's ministry. He also begins to reveal to his readers who Jesus is by his description of Jesus' baptism, temptation, and early preaching and healing ministry in Galilee.

DISCUSSION 2—MARK 2:1-28; 3:1-6

Controversy

In this section a reaction of criticism and opposition to Jesus' words and actions begins to set in.

Mark 2:1-12

(1) Where and why does the crowd gather? What has Jesus done previously in Capernaum?

(2) What indications of Jesus' popularity are there at this time?

(3) Why and how is Jesus' preaching interrupted? What is his reaction to this interruption?

(4) What do you think the paralytic's friends have in mind? Compare with what Jesus says in verse 5.

(5) Who reacts to this statement? How do they react? Why? Look up "scribes" and "blasphemy" in a collegiate dictionary.

(Note—Under Jewish law, blasphemy was punishable by death.)

(6) In your own words what are the scribes saying? How does Jesus answer? What is the point of Jesus' question in verse 9?

(7) What does Jesus expect to prove to the scribes by healing the paralytic?

(8) How does the paralytic express his faith? What are the reactions to his healing? With whom do the people connect the healing?

Mark 2:13-17

(9) Who now joins the four fishermen as a disciple of Jesus? How does Levi introduce Jesus to his friends? Tax collectors were despised as thieves and collaborators with Rome.

(10) Who complains, to whom, about what? How does Jesus handle this complaint? What claim does he make about himself? What is he saying about the Pharisees?

Mark 2:18-22

(11) Why are Jesus' disciples criticized? What is the point of his illustration about the bridegroom? Since one purpose of fasting is to bring us closer to God, why do Jesus' disciples not need to fast for a while?

(12) In the parallel illustrations in verses 21, 22 what similarities are there? What are both illustrations saying? What conformity to the "old " is at issue in verse 18?

Mark 2:23-28

(13) What new element comes into the Pharisees' exchanges with Jesus?

(14) How does Jesus deal with their new complaint? To what does he appeal? What does Jesus explain about the purpose of the Sabbath? What claim does he make for himself?

(Note—"Son of man" is the name Jesus uses in referring to himself. See Mark 2:10. At this time there were over a thousand man-made rules and regulations concerning the Sabbath, making the Sabbath which had been given for man's physical and spiritual benefit a terrible burden to him.)

Mark 3:1-6

(15) What change do you observe in those who oppose Jesus? What is the setting for this incident?

(16) What does verse 3 reveal about Jesus? Why don't they respond to his question? Why is Jesus disturbed?

(17) What are the results of this healing?

(Note—The Pharisees and Herodians normally would have nothing to do with each other.)

SUMMARY

(1) Trace the increasing degree of opposition to Jesus through each of these five sections. From whom does opposition arise, and for what reasons? Who opposes Jesus today, and why?

(2) What claims does Jesus make in Mark 2:1—3:6? How do they affect you?

(3) Consider what happens to the paralytic, to Levi, and to the man with the withered hand when they meet Jesus. Why is their experience so different from that of the Pharisees?

CONCLUSION

Jesus said and did things that made some people react negatively. His claims of authority and his lack of conformity to the religious status quo disturbed the religious leaders of his day to the point that early in Jesus' ministry they wanted to destroy him.

Authority Questioned

This portion provides a continuing example of the contrasting reactions to Jesus found in chapters 1 and 2. Jesus cut a deep channel in society and people reacted strongly for or against him.

Mark 3:7-12

(1) Compare 3:7 with 2:13. What reasons might Jesus have for choosing the seaside for his teaching?

(2) How does Mark emphasize the size of the crowds which are following Jesus? Consult your map and locate the areas from which the crowds come. How far-reaching is his ministry? Compare with Mark 1:28.

(3) Why is Jesus drawing such large groups?

(4) What pattern in dealing with unclean spirits emerges in verses 11, 12? How does this compare with the first recorded incident of Jesus' dealing with an unclean spirit in Mark 1:23-26?

(5) Why would Jesus not want publicity from the unclean spirits?

Mark 3:13-19

(6) For what three purposes are the twelve appointed? What is significant about the order in which these three things are mentioned?

(7) To which three disciples does Jesus give additional names? To whom do we usually give nicknames? What does "sons of thunder" suggest about the personalities of James and John? Watch for times later in the narrative when Peter, James and John appear as a select group.

(8) What other special notations are made about the disciples?

Mark 3:20-30

(9) Why doesn't Jesus have time to eat? What do his friends think about this?

(10) From where have the scribes come who accuse Jesus? What is their accusation? Why? (What things

has Jesus done which require supernatural power? What do the scribes say is the source of Jesus' power?)

(11) How does Jesus rule their accusation as illogical by the use of the three "if" clauses in verses 24-26?

(12) What further claim is Jesus making in verse 27? Who is the strong man whose house is being plundered? (Note—Jesus has been driving out Satan's demons.)

(13) What indictment does Jesus make against his accusers? How have they blasphemed against the Holy Spirit? See verse 30. (What is the source of Jesus' power? Mark 1:10, 11. What do the scribes say is the source of his power?)

(14) What are the works of Jesus meant to reveal? What do his accusers say they reveal? (God only deals with men by the Holy Spirit. As long as a man says the goodness of God is the evil of Satan, he will not come to God, repent and receive God's forgiveness. He cuts himself off from the only avenue to God.)

Mark 3:31-35

(15) Describe the scene in this paragraph.

(16) What does Jesus teach is the basis of a relationship with him? What does *whosoever* mean? How are those here to whom he speaks meeting the requirement?

SUMMARY

(1) In this section what effects, positive and negative, result from Jesus' activities in chapters 1 and 2?

(2) If you were one of the twelve disciples, what warning and what challenge would you remember from what happens in verses 20-35? How does this warning and this challenge apply to you?

CONCLUSION

Like a stone flung into a pool of water, the ministry of Jesus is having increasing repercussions. The crowd squeezed into a home (Mark 2:2) has become a great multitude (3:7 and following). The opposition which took the form of questioning in the heart (2:6) has now become an open accusation of Satanic activity. Worthy of note in this section is Jesus' statement that anyone may have a close personal relationship to him based not on physical ties but on doing the will of God.

DISCUSSION 4—MARK 4:1-34

Parables

Webster's Dictionary defines *parable* as "a comparison; specifically, a short fictitious narrative, from which a moral or spiritual truth is drawn." In this chapter there is a series of parables which Jesus used to teach his listeners. The Jewish people of Jesus' day were accustomed to being taught in parables. Teachers and audiences both were familiar with this teaching method.

Mark 4:1-9

(1) If you were an artist how would you paint the scene in verse 1? What are the advantages of holding a teaching session in this manner?

(2) In verses 3 and 9 how does Jesus begin and conclude his parable? Put in your own words what he is emphasizing here.

(3) Describe briefly the four kinds of soil which receive the seed in this parable.

Mark 4:10-20

(4) Who receives Jesus' interpretation of this parable? Why? What does Jesus say that their concern about the meaning of the parable indicates (verse 11)? Check verse 10 again to see who has made the division between those inside and outside.

(5) What happens to those outside who hear the parables?

(Note—Verse 12 is a quotation from Isaiah 6:9, 10. William Barclay comments, "The Greek version (of Isaiah 6:9, 10) does not say that God intended that the people should be so dull that they would not understand; it says that they had made themselves so dull that they could not understand—which is a very different thing.")

(6) How does Jesus identify the seed in the parable? Describe in your own words each of the four kinds of people mentioned. What experience do they share (verses 15, 16, 18, 20)? In what ways do they differ from one another?

(7) What specific kind of pressure undermines the faith

of the people described in verses 16, 17? Relate your own experience of such pressure.

(8) What three types of things prevent the people in verses 18, 19 from being fruitful? Give a present-day example of each of these three things.

(9) What variation occurs even among people who are good soil for the reception of God's word? Since each of the four types of people in this parable *hear* the word, what makes the difference in their lives?

Mark 4:21-25

(10) What similar thought is expressed both in verses 21 and 22? Where has Jesus mentioned "secret" before in this chapter? (Verse 11, in referring to the meaning of his parables) If Jesus in verses 21, 22 is referring to the purpose of parables, what does he say about them?

(11) Compare verse 23 with verse 9, noting the immediate context. How does Jesus go on in verses 24, 25 to emphasize the importance of paying attention, of listening to the word of God? What happens when we cease to give it our attention?

Mark 4:26-34

(12) What understanding does Jesus seek to give us in the parable in verses 26-29? What things does this parable teach about the growth of the kingdom of God?

(13) At what point is the growth hidden, at what point is it obvious? How does this parable apply to the growth of the kingdom of God within an individual? How does it apply if we think in terms of the kingdom of God abroad in the world throughout all generations?

(14) What is the main point of the parable in verses 30-32? If you start with the smallest and finish with the greatest, what does this indicate about the rate of growth?

How does this parable apply to the kingdom of God's growth in an individual? How does it apply to the growth of the kingdom of God in the world? Compare the extent of Christ's ministry at this point in Mark's Gospel with its extent today.

(15) What do verses 33. 34 reveal about Jesus' pattern of teaching?

(Note—The word "disciples" in Mark refers to a larger group than the twelve.)

SUMMARY

(1) From this chapter what specific impressions do you have of Jesus' teaching?

(2) Why, do you think, does Jesus emphasize the importance of the way in which we hear, the attention and response we give, to the word of God?

(3) In Mark 1:15 Jesus' early preaching is described. What do the parables in this chapter add to his teaching about the kingdom of God?

CONCLUSION

Listening to the teachings of Jesus is not enough. Hearing must be followed by obedience. The word of God must be allowed to take root, grow, and bear fruit in our lives.

DISCUSSION 5—MARK 4:35-41; 5:1-43

The Desperate Ones

In this section Mark returns to his narrative and relates four incidents in which Jesus is confronted with extremely difficult situations, two of which are emergencies.

Mark 4:35-41

(1) What "day" is Mark referring to? When do they leave? Who suggests the trip? What indicates that the trip is impromptu?

(2) The sea of Galilee is known for its violent storms which arise with frightening swiftness. How does Mark emphasize the violence of this storm?

(3) Why is Jesus asleep? What has he been doing all day? Who probably is in charge of the boat? (See Mark 1:16-20.) Why do they wake Jesus? What does their question to him imply?

(4) How does Jesus deal with the situation? How do his action and his two questions to the disciples answer their question of verse 38?

(5) Why does this incident seem to make a deeper impression on the disciples than anything they have thus far witnessed?

Mark 5:1-20

The fact that this incident takes place on the eastern shore of the sea of Galilee indicates it is Gentile territory, which probably accounts for some of the things Jesus does differently here.

(6) What do you learn about the man's condition from verses 3-5? How would the people of the countryside feel about him?

(7) According to verse 8, who is doing the speaking in verse 7? Compare with Mark 1:24, 34 and 3:11, 12. What insight do these spirits invariably seem to have?

(8) From verses 8-13 what new things do you learn about unclean spirits?

(9) What three changes take place in the demoniac? How do the people react? Why? What is their reaction to Jesus when they realize his power? Contrast the demoniac's reaction. How do people today react to Jesus' power in these two ways?

(10) What commission does Jesus give to this man? (Remember that the demoniac lives in Gentile territory where Jesus is not having a continuing ministry.) Compare with Jesus' charge to the leper in Mark 1:40-45. How does each comply?

Mark 5:21-24

(11) Jesus does not remain in Gentile territory. Where does he go?

(12) Who is Jairus and what is his need? What does he want Jesus to do? What faith does he have?

Mark 5:25-34

(13) Describe the scene in this paragraph as you see it in your imagination.

(14) What specific things do you know about this woman's condition? What do you learn about the physicians of her day? Do people today still have such experiences? How do they feel?

(15) What does the woman know about Jesus? What does she believe? What happens? Why would she seek healing in this way rather than coming forward with her request as Jairus did?

(Note—Under the laws of Judaism this woman's condition made her ceremonially unclean, and everyone who touched her would be considered unclean. (Leviticus 15:25-27). Her illness thus shut her off from worship in the temple and ordinary social life.)

(16) What do verses 30, 31, indicate about the two ways in which it is possible to touch Jesus? What made the difference in the woman's touch? How is it possible for people today to have only a superficial contact with Jesus?

(17) Why is the woman so fearful in verse 33? What does her interview with Jesus do for her? What does she gain besides healing?

Mark 5:35-43

(18) Imagine yourself as Jairus. How do you feel as Jesus talks with the woman? How do you feel when the messenger comes?

(19) In essence, what claim is Jesus making in verse 36? What does he require of Jairus? Compare Jairus' reaction to Jesus' claim with the reaction of the mourners.

(20) Who are the five witnesses to the healing? What instructions does Jesus give? How would his instructions help them to overcome their awe and to regard the girl as a normal twelve year old and not a ghost?

SUMMARY

(1) Over what forces does Jesus exhibit his power and authority in today's study? What are the various reactions to his power?

(2) What responses does Jesus desire from those who come into contact with him?

CONCLUSION

In chapter 4 the disciples learned through parables. In this section they learn through actual experience in desperate situations. In the storm at sea they realize that the one whom they follow can control the forces of nature. Then they see his power to cast out evil spirits which were destroying a man's mind and personality. They see his power to heal a woman's chronic incurable disease, and to restore life to a dead child. They see that Jesus' power and concern affect every area of human need.

DISCUSSION 6—MARK 6

Death of John the Baptist
Feeding the Five Thousand

This chapter gives us some insight into what was involved in being a disciple or follower of Jesus during his earthly ministry. The privileges, responsibilities and difficulties encountered by these first disciples may be translated into our own situations.

Mark 6:1-6

(1) Describe this incident as to place, people present, their actions and reactions.

(2) What is at the root of the townspeople's attitude? How does their unbelief affect Jesus' ministry among them?

Mark 6:7-13

(3) What authority and what special orders does Jesus give the twelve? What reasons could there be to travel light, to stay in only one home in a village, to leave a place which rejects their message?

(4) Compare the message the disciples preach with John's message (Mark 1:4) and Jesus' message (1:15). What do the disciples do in addition to preaching? Where do they get this power? How will their ministry help to spread Jesus' message?

Mark 6:14-29

(5) Who learns of the work of these six teams? What are some of the common statements regarding Jesus' identity? (Notice that in Mark 4:41 even the disciples of Jesus wonder who he is.)

(6) How has Herod identified Jesus? Why? Why did Herod arrest John the Baptist? How did he feel toward John? Why did he put John to death?

Why did Herod fail to accept John's message? What things today keep people from obeying God's commands?

Mark 6:30-44

(7) Imagine how the disciples feel now that they have returned from their trips. What does Jesus suggest? What ruins their plans for a day off?

(8) Describe the scene in verses 32-34.

(9) How does Jesus react to this interruption in plans? What does he see as the need of this crowd?

(10) At what point do the disciples want Jesus to get rid of the crowd? What reason do they give? How must they feel at this point? What challenge does Jesus give his disciples? How do they react?

(11) What indicates that the disciples have not considered their resources? How does Jesus use what they have? What jobs does he give the disciples? Compare this with what they originally had in mind for the day's activities.

Mark 6:45-52

(12) See John 6:15 to discover the reaction of the people to this miracle. Why would Jesus not want his disciples to stay where the people intended this?

(13) Where does Jesus go? What does he do, and why?

(14) How is the disciples' day of frustration progressing by the fourth watch (3 a.m.)? Describe this incident including Jesus' actions and the disciples' actions and reactions. Considering what has been involved for them on this day, what may be the explanation for the hardness of their hearts?

(15) We tend to think that if trouble comes to us it must mean we are not doing God's will. How did Jesus' disciples get into this distressing situation on the sea?

Mark 6:53-56

(16) What does the stop at Gennesaret reveal? How has the experience of the woman with the flow of blood affected Jesus' ministry? Why is Jesus continuing to be so popular with the crowds?

SUMMARY

(1) What demands are made upon Jesus' disciples in this chapter? What indicates that Jesus does not expect his followers always to receive a welcome and a hearing?

(2) What feeling does Jesus have for the crowds which his disciples apparently do not share? How can we learn to have Jesus' compassion for people?

CONCLUSION

In this chapter there are three examples of people who failed to receive spiritual truth. Influenced by a surface familiarity with Jesus which led to unbelief, the people in his home area did not see him do any mighty work in their midst. Herod misunderstood who Jesus was because he had failed to act on John the Baptist's message. Even Jesus' disciples, though they had recently experienced his power in their own ministry, did not grasp the meaning of his power revealed in the feeding of the 5,000, and they were completely astounded when Jesus came walking to them on the water.

DISCUSSION 7—MARK 7

Tradition or The Word of God

Here we have one of the major clashes between Jesus and the Pharisees. Jesus uses their practice of Corban as one example of their spiritual corruption.

(Note—By pronouncing Corban (verse 11) on a piece of property or money a person announced that it was now given and dedicated to God, which relieved the man from using it for anyone else, although it might be kept in his own possession until his death.)

Mark 7:1-8

(1) What gives rise to the discussion which begins in verse 5? Why are these men particularly alert to the traditions of the elders? For them what is the standard of purity here? Note that the disciples were eating with hands which were *ceremonially* defiled.

(2) How does Jesus handle the criticism? What accusation does he make? What is the point of the quotation from Isaiah? What choice does Jesus say the Pharisees have made?

(Note—The New Bible Dictionary says regarding Jewish tradition, "The word (tradition) does not occur in the Old Testament but between the Testaments much teaching in elaboration and explanation of the Old Testament was added by the Rabbis. This was handed down from teacher to pupil, and by our Lord's day had assumed a place alongside the Scripture in importance. This equation of human commentary with divine revelation was condemned by our Lord.")

Mark 7:9-13

(3) How does Jesus go on to illustrate the point he makes in verses 6-8?

(4) What contrast is drawn between what Moses said and what they say?

(5) What verbs does Jesus contrast in verses 8, 9, 13 to indicate the position of the Pharisees? What indicates that Corban is only one illustration of their spiritual condition?

(6) How do the Pharisees judge their own and others' righteousness or standing before God?

Mark 7:14-23

(7) To whom is this paragraph addressed? What shows that Jesus considers this teaching important?

(8) What is the source of defilement (verse 15)? What do the Pharisees consider to be the source of defilement (verses 1-5)?

(9) What further teaching do the disciples receive? Why? Compare with Mark 4:10.

(10) What is true defilement? What is its source? How does Jesus' teaching here go contrary to what the Jews believed? What is first on the list of that which comes out of a man and makes him unclean? What other things follow? Discuss the meaning of each. (Foolishness is moral folly or treating sin as a joke.)

(11) Why is Jesus' analysis of man's condition as valid today as the day he said it?

(12) How do you know that Jesus did not agree with the Pharisees' belief that a man could be considered righteous by performing certain religious rituals? Why is the problem much deeper? What kind of cure will have to be found?

Mark 7:24-30

(13) Locate Tyre and Sidon. What apparently is Jesus' purpose in going so far into Gentile territory? Compare Mark 6:31.

(14) What do you learn about the woman? (Note— Greek indicates her religion and Syrophoenician her nationality.) Why does she come to Jesus? What do you observe about the way in which she comes?

(15) How would you explain Jesus' response to her request? Remember, tone of voice makes a big difference in the effect of what we say. In verse 27 what does the word "first" suggest?

(Note—"Children" here refers to Israel which was to receive the first offer of the gospel. The word used for dogs suggests the household pets, an affectionate term.)

(16) How would you characterize the woman's response? What suggests boldness and what suggests humility on her part? How does Jesus evaluate her response? What unusual element appears in this healing? (Where is the person who is healed?)

Mark 7:31-37

(17) What contrasts do you observe between this paragraph and the previous one? What difference is there in location, problem, and who initiates the interview?

(18) What are the specific stages in the healing of this man? How would Jesus' actions begin to develop faith in the man? Why may the deaf man not have been involved in the faith which brought him to Jesus?

(19) What three things does the deaf man experience (verse 35)?

(20) Compare the request in verse 32 with the request in verse 36. Who makes each request and what is the response in each case? Why is the people's response to Jesus' request inconsistent with their words in verse 37?

SUMMARY

(1) According to Jesus' teaching in the first half of this chapter, what is man's basic problem? How does Jesus define hypocrisy?

(2) In the two incidents of healing what kind of response does Jesus seek and approve?

CONCLUSION

If a man's defilement is not an outward matter and cannot be treated by outward measures, his right standing with God cannot depend upon ritual or works. Only that which deals with the heart of man and treats the inner defilement will be sufficient to handle the problem.

DISCUSSION 8—MARK 8:1-38; 9:1

You Are the Christ!

In this chapter we come to the turning point of the book. In it we find the second mention of the title "Christ," the first being in Mark 1:1. Jesus' major Galilean ministry has come to an end and he turns toward Jerusalem. A new element and emphasis enters Jesus' teaching to his disciples.

Mark 8:1-10

(1) At first reading this incident seems to be the same as that described in Mark 6:30-44, but what are the distinct differences?

What was Jesus' attitude toward the people and their needs in each incident? What is the extent of your concern for the spiritual and physical needs of others? How do you express this concern?

Mark 8:11-21

(2) In verses 11-13 what sort of sign may the Pharisees have in mind? What do we show about ourselves when we seek a sign?

(3) How does Jesus respond to the Pharisees at this point? Why?

(4) Considering the former interviews between Jesus and the Pharisees, why have they now apparently reached an impasse?

(5) Explain the warning Jesus gives to his disciples in verse 15. What attitude was typical of the Pharisees (Mark 7)? What attitude or way of life was typical of Herod (Mark 6)? How are these opposite ways of life equally dangerous?

(6) About what are the disciples worried? What does Jesus try to make them recognize by his series of questions?

Mark 8:22-26

(7) Why, do you think, did Jesus heal this man in stages? Who initiated the incident? How did Jesus get the man himself involved in the healing? How was faith stimulated here?

Mark 8:27-33

(8) Locate the place Jesus now takes his disciples. Why would he go this far north? Compare with Mark 7:24.

(9) What two questions does Jesus now put to his disciples? What is the significant difference between the two questions? If Jesus asked you both of these questions today, how would you answer each?

(10) How do the disciples answer the first question? Note how the question of Jesus' identity is primary in Mark's Gospel. See for example Mark 1:11, 24; 3:11; 4:41; 6:2, 3, 14, 15.

(11) How does Peter, speaking for the group, answer Jesus' second question?

(12) Upon the disciples' confession of belief that he is the Christ, the Messiah, what does Jesus now for the first time begin to teach them concerning the Messiah? What four specific things does he mention? What indicates that Jesus does not at this point teach in parables?

(13) How does Peter react to this teaching? Why? What hopes must Peter and the others have?

(14) How does Mark describe Jesus' reaction in verse 33? What indicates that the situation is ripe with temptation for Jesus?

(15) Why is Peter's response to Jesus' teaching about his death man's point of view rather than God's point of view?

Mark 8:34—9:1

(16) To whom does Jesus direct this paragraph? What do the words "whoever" and "if any man" indicate?

(17) What does verse 34 teach about the cost of discipleship? What does it mean to deny one*self*? (It does

not say to deny yourself *things,* but to deny your*self.*) What are the other two requirements of discipleship?

(Note—This is the first time the cross is mentioned in Mark's Gospel. At the time of Jesus, it meant the instrument of public execution by the Romans.)

(18) In verse 35 what two possibilities does Jesus state are open to every man? Why does either way involve losing your life? What is the difference? What is the only way to save your life?

(19) How do verses 36, 37 strengthen Jesus' argument? What is the best that man living for self can do? With what result? (When Alexander the Great had conquered the empires of his day, he wept that there were no more worlds to conquer.)

(20) What reaction may some people have to Jesus and to his words, according to verse 38? Why would the cross involve shame?

How is Jesus' prophecy of his return in power and glory both a warning and an encouragement to those hearing his words?

SUMMARY

(1) What things have led the disciples to conclude that Jesus is the Christ (the Messiah)?

(2) What demand does Jesus now make of them? Why is commitment only the first step of true discipleship?

(3) What major elements of the Apostles' Creed are mentioned in this chapter?

CONCLUSION

Since the events of chapter 6, Jesus has been trying to get away from the multitudes in order to give some special teaching to his disciples. It is to them he puts the challenge of his identity and gives the teaching concerning his death and resurrection.

This page may be used for study notes.

DISCUSSION 9—REVIEW OF MARK 1—8

Review

In preparation for the review discussion, each person in the group should read Mark, chapters one through eight, during the week before the discussion. As you read, *look* for what these eight chapters reveal about Jesus and his identity. Discover what he says, what he does, and what others say about him. Try to get an *overall view* of the first half of the book. Follow through the major themes or ideas.

Each person in the group should choose *one* of the review questions for special study and prepare to lead the group in consideration of that question during the discussion.

(1) Describe the ministry of John the Baptist. What is the core of his message and the effect of his ministry? How does he identify Jesus? How does Mark's Gospel connect John with the Old Testament prophecy of Messiah?

(2) What does Jesus teach in these chapters about who he is, about his mission, about his own destiny?

(3) What does Jesus teach about the kingdom of God? about the Sabbath? about the nature of defilement? about being his disciple?

(4) What does Jesus reveal about himself through his dealings with individuals and with groups? (What emotions does he exhibit? What sorts of things does he do, and what do they indicate about his character?) Give specific examples.

(5) Describe Jesus' disciples. What do they see? What do they learn? How do they react in specific situations? What do they come to believe about Jesus? Trace the progress of their faith.

(6) How do individuals other than his disciples react to Jesus? What positive and what negative reactions are described? How do you account for the varying attitudes these people have toward Jesus?

(7) From the evidence thus far presented in Mark's Gospel, what conclusion have you reached as to Jesus' identity and the source of his power and authority?

DISCUSSION 10—MARK 9:2-50

The Transfiguration Belief and Unbelief

The disciples receive a number of revelations in this chapter. They face several things which they find it difficult to understand. Jesus gives them teachings more severe in nature than before, and he begins his journey southward toward Jerusalem and the day when he will be parted from his disciples.

Mark 9:2-13

(1) Describe this event known as the transfiguration. When and where does it take place? Who are the witnesses? To what other unique event have these three men been witness (5:37-43)?

How would the transfiguration confirm to the disciples the rightness of their confession in Mark 8:29?

(2) How do you account for Peter's reaction (verse 5)? What does the voice from the cloud say?

(3) What time limit does Jesus set on the command he gives the three? What two questions do they have? They refer to the authority of the scribes in their second question. To what authority and to what subject does Jesus direct them in his answer? To what authority should we direct those who question us on theological matters?

(4) Concerning Elijah, compare Mark 9:11-13 with Matthew 17:10-13.

Mark 9:14-29

(5) During Jesus' time on the mountain with Peter, James and John, what is happening to the other disciples? What frustration has come to them? What are they doing about it?

(6) How has the disciples' failure affected this father's faith (verses 17, 18, 22)? From verses 19, 23 what does Jesus see as the basic problem in all those involved here?

(7) What happens to the boy as he is brought to Jesus? Why, do you think, does Jesus discuss the boy's condition with the father? How does the father respond to Jesus' challenge to believe him? How does Jesus answer this request?

(8) Consider the steps in this man's experience from the time he brought his son to the disciples until the boy is healed. How does this parallel the experience of some today who find the followers of Jesus inadequate? What does such a person need?

(9) Analyze what happened to the disciples in this episode. According to Jesus' diagnosis, why were they unable to handle the situation? What were they doing (verse 14) instead of praying? About what, do you think, were they arguing with the scribes? Rather than arguing about reasons for our ineffectiveness as Christians, what ought we to do (verses 28, 29)?

Mark 9:30-41

(10) Why does Jesus wish to keep his travels a secret at this point? What is the reaction of the disciples to Jesus' teaching?

(11) Compare the subject of concern in Jesus' mind (verse 31) with that in the disciples' minds (verses 33, 34). How do the disciples feel when Jesus inquires about their discussion? Why? What events in this chapter may have led to the disciples' discussion?

(12) What is the two-fold teaching of verses 35-37? What does it mean to receive someone *in Jesus' name?*

(13) Of what is John reminded by Jesus' remark in verse 37? Why did the disciples censure this man? What further insight does this give you into the disciples' attitudes at this point? How may the incident with the deaf and dumb spirit have contributed to their attitude?

(14) What is Jesus' response to John's statement? What does Jesus teach about God's evaluation of deeds? What promise does he make?

(15) Why is a man judged solely on the basis of his relationship to Jesus Christ? Notice the emphasis on Jesus' *name* in verses 37-39, 41. What does it mean to do something in someone's name?

Mark 9:42-50

(16) In verses 42-47 there are four comparative statements. In each case what is *better* than what?

(17) In the first example what warning is given concerning our relationship with others? Who are the little ones? In today's society what forms may the stumbling-block take which causes others to sin?

(18) How can one's hand or foot or eye cause him to sin? What is the consequence of sin in each case, and what is preferable to this (verses 43-47)?

What spiritual truth is Jesus teaching by the use of this vivid pictorial language?

(19) What is the purpose and value of salt? When is salt useless? What is the meaning of the two commands Jesus gives his disciples (verse 50)?

SUMMARY

(1) Sum up the main teachings which Jesus gives to his disciples in this chapter. What do the disciples learn about Jesus, about themselves, about others?

(2) Discuss how you can apply to your own lives the teachings of this chapter about sin and about good works.

CONCLUSION

In this chapter we see the contrast between the mind of Jesus and the mind of the disciples, a contrast that emphasizes how alone Jesus was as he faced the cross. In the disciples we see a reflection of our own experiences. Even as followers of Jesus we lack understanding, we put confidence in religious leaders rather than in Scripture. We are frustrated and defensive when we are without power spiritually, fearful, and concerned for our own position.

DISCUSSION 11—MARK 10

Questions

In this chapter the events which immediately precede Holy Week are recounted. Jesus continues his journey toward Jerusalem. On the way five different groups or individuals come to him with requests. Of these five (the Pharisees, the children, the rich man, James and John, Bartimaeus) only two ask aright and receive what they want. A thoughtful study of this chapter will teach us much about ourselves.

Mark 10:1-12

(1) By whom and for what purpose is Jesus questioned? Why are the Pharisees in particular concerned with matters of law? How does Jesus explain Moses' treatment of divorce? (It should be noted that Moses' teaching was not to provide opportunity to divorce but to curb a bad situation and to provide some rule and order in this matter.)

(2) What does Jesus emphasize as the plan of God concerning marriage? According to verse 9, whose work is being destroyed by divorce? Why is fidelity, rather than "love," the chief virtue of the marriage relationship?

(3) What further teaching does Jesus give to the disciples on this matter? How do you know that Jesus does not hold to a different standard for men and women?

Mark 10:13-16

(4) Why would the disciples rebuke those bringing children to Jesus? How does Jesus use this incident to teach his disciples about the kingdom of God? What does it mean to receive like a child?

Mark 10:17-31

(5) What do you learn about the man in verses 17-22? What does he think about Jesus? What lack does he sense in his own life? What does the verb "do" (verse 17) tell about his thinking concerning eternal life?

(6) What claim is Jesus making in verse 18? How may this also be a challenge to the man's estimate of himself? From the man's claim in verse 20 what does he think of himself?

(7) See Exodus 20:3-17. Which commandments does Jesus not mention? With what relationship do the commandments not mentioned have to do? Those mentioned concern what relationship?

Why would it be relatively easy for a rich man to keep the commands mentioned? How do you know this man is telling the truth?

(8) What are the two parts of the command Jesus gives the man? What does his failure to obey reveal about the one thing he lacks? How does he fail in regard to the commandments not mentioned? What is his god? What does he value above treasure in heaven?

(9) How does Jesus startle his disciples? (Remember that the Jews of that day felt that wealth was an indication of God's favor and blessing.) Why is it hard for those who have riches to enter the kingdom of God? What riches do you have, and how may they stand in your way? How *is* salvation possible?

(10) What does Peter claim for himself and the others? What does Jesus promise? Why can we never say that God is in our debt?

To whom do the promises of verses 29, 30 apply? Does Jesus offer his followers a bed of roses? Give examples of how the promises in verses 29, 30 have been fulfilled in the lives of people today.

Mark 10:32-34

(11) What new details does Jesus give to the twelve concerning the events which lie ahead? Compare with Mark 8:31 and 9:31. What basic elements appear each time?

Mark 10:35-45

(12) Compare what Jesus has on his mind (verses 32-34) with what concerns James and John (verses 35-45). Put their request in your own words. How does Jesus answer their request (verses 38-40)? Why?

(13) What indicates the self-confidence of the two

brothers? What shows that the attitude of the other disciples is no better than that of James and John? Compare
10:41 with 9:34.

(14) What contrast does Jesus draw in verses 42-44?
How is he himself the supreme example?

(15) Why is it essential for the disciples to understand
true greatness in the spiritual realm?

(16) Verse 45 is considered the key verse of the Gospel
of Mark. How does what you have studied thus far in Mark
illustrate the first half of verse 45?

What is the ultimate purpose of Jesus' coming? What
does the word *ransom* indicate? What does this verse reveal for the first time in Mark's Gospel about Jesus'
death?

Mark 10:46-52

(17) What is Bartimaeus' request (verses 47, 48)?
Compare it with the request of James and John in verse
37. Why does Jesus ask Bartimaeus specifically what he
wants?

(18) Why is Bartimaeus healed? What does he do
afterward? Why is mercy the one request that is always
answered by the Lord? What do we indicate when we ask
for mercy?

SUMMARY

(1) How does Jesus answer those who put confidence
in a legalistic approach to life (verses 2-9)?

(2) What is Jesus' challenge to those who put their confidence in material things (verses 17-22)?

(3) What is Jesus' teaching to those who put their confidence in earthly position and power (verses 35-45)?

(4) What is necessary to obtain eternal life (to enter
the kingdom of God)?

CONCLUSION

The only people in this chapter who receive their requests from Jesus are the children and Bartimaeus. The
former desire his touch, the latter his mercy. We may
have confidence of Jesus' answer if we make these same
requests of him.

DISCUSSION 12—MARK 11

Triumphal Entry

The events of Sunday, Monday and part of Tuesday in Holy Week are recounted in this chapter. These events are centered in and around Jerusalem, the headquarters of the Pharisees who are seeking to destroy Jesus.

Mark 11:1-11

(1) What instructions does Jesus give to two of his disciples? What indicates that Jesus himself is initiating the triumphal entry?

(Note—Riding on the colt was not a sign of humility but rather the sign of a royal person coming in peace rather than war.)

(2) How do the people react to Jesus' entry into Jerusalem? What do they do? What do they say? According to verse 10, to what do the people look forward? Many of them, no doubt, think in terms of a Messiah who will overthrow the yoke of Rome.

(3) Instead of organizing an overthrow of Rome, what is Jesus' first act after his entry into Jerusalem? With what is he concerned? Where do Jesus and the twelve go to spend the night? Why may this be a safety move? See 14:1.

Mark 11:12-26

(4) What happens on the way back into Jerusalem on the following morning?

(Note—This is a difficult paragraph. Some scholars feel that it is an enacted parable which warns against show (profession) without reality. This may point directly to Israel and the temple worship in particular. Other scholars indicate that though it was not yet the season for full fruit there would be the early crop of green knobs or immature fruit which appear before the leaves if the tree is going to bear fruit later. This early fruit was sometimes eaten by the traveler. The lack of any fruit at this point meant that there would be no mature fruit in season and that the leaves were a deception.)

(5) Describe the events in the temple. If you had been a witness here, what would you have seen and heard? What apparently are the disciples doing?

What impression do you get of Jesus here? What reason does he give for his action? What does the phrase "all nations" imply?

How would the profiteering in animals and in currency exchange in the temple affect those who come truly desiring to worship God?

(6) What reaction is there to Jesus' expression of authority in cleansing the temple? Why is he feared by his enemies? How do Jesus' actions here compare with the expectations of many that Messiah would exercise political authority?

(7) What pattern do Jesus and the twelve follow each evening?

(8) How does the fig tree (verse 20) now conform outwardly to what it is inwardly?

(9) What teaching does Jesus give the disciples upon this occasion? What do such words as *whoever, whatever,* and *whenever* indicate about the scope of the statements which Jesus is making? What conditions must be fulfilled in order to receive answers to prayer?

(10) Why is it essential that we focus our attention on the greatness of God rather than on the size of our mountains when we pray? Peter has been impressed with the withering of the fig tree and Jesus says that even mountains are subject to God.

(11) What element besides requests is basic in prayer? Why? Why can not we pray properly with an unforgiving spirit?

Mark 11:27-33

(12) Where does this conversation take place? Who initiates it? Why? What *things* do Jesus' questioners refer to? See verses 15-17. Put their questions into your own words.

(13) How does Jesus answer their questions? Why can't they answer his question about John? What did John proclaim about Jesus? See John 1:19-34. How would this have answered their question about the authority of

Jesus? Why can't they simply ignore John the Baptist's ministry?

(14) What did John's baptism signify? See Mark 1:4. Why is repentance essential as a condition for accepting the authority and lordship of Jesus?

SUMMARY

(1) What does Jesus reveal about himself once he arrives in Jerusalem? What claims is he making by his actions? What various reactions are there to these claims?

(2) In verses 17, 23-25 Jesus indicates his concern with prayer in several of its many aspects. Discuss how his teachings in this chapter about prayer may be applied practically to your own praying.

CONCLUSION

Starting with this chapter, Mark devotes the remainder of his Gospel to a detailed account of the last week of Jesus' earthly life. Because much of the action now centers in the temple, everything Jesus says and does has almost immediate repercussions. Jesus' claims and actions are becoming more and more pointed, as the triumphal entry and the cleansing of the temple illustrate.

DISCUSSION 13—MARK 12

Teaching in the Temple

The questions in the temple which began in Mark 11:27 continue throughout chapter 12. The first paragraph of this chapter is a continuation of Jesus' answer to the question of his authority.

Mark 12:1-12

(1) What is the point of this parable (verses 1-9)? How do the tenants treat the servants? How is the owner's son described? How is the son's authority received?

(2) What prophecy does Jesus make in the parable?

(Note—In this parable the owner of the vineyard is God, the vineyard is Israel and the tenants are the rulers of Israel. The servants are the prophets and the son is Jesus himself.)

(3) How does Jesus' quotation from the Old Testament repeat the main point of the parable using a different picture? Who are the builders and who is the rejected cornerstone?

(4) What is the reaction of the chief priests, scribes and elders to this parable? Why? How has Jesus answered their original question (11:28)?

Mark 12:13-17

(5) With what motive and what manner do the Pharisees and the Herodians come to Jesus? Why would they believe that their question is a perfect trap? What would happen if Jesus were to answer "yes"? "no"?

(6) What does Jesus recognize about his questioners? Compare with Mark 7:6. What is hypocrisy?

(7) How does Jesus answer their question? What things are Caesar's? What things are God's? To what situations may this principle be rightly applied today?

(8) Why is this delegation sent to trap Jesus so amazed at him?

Mark 12:18-27

(9) What characterizes the next group that questions Jesus? What does their position concerning the resurrection reveal about their question? To what authority do they refer? What is their question?

(10) On what two subjects does Jesus say the Sadducees are wrong? Why? Of what are they ignorant? To what authority does Jesus appeal?

(11) What Scripture and what reasoning does Jesus use to prove that there is a resurrection?

Mark 12:28-34

(12) What stimulates the next question? What does this indicate about the religious leadership in Israel? What is the meaning of the scribe's question?

(13) Analyze Jesus' answer in verses 29-31. In what way is Jesus' answer a summation of the ten commandments? (See Exodus 20:3-17 for the ten commandments.)

Note that Jesus' answer is a quotation from two other portions of the Old Testament (Deuteronomy 6:4, 5; Leviticus 19:18).

(14) What, do you think, does it mean to love the Lord your God in the way which Jesus describes? What does it mean to love your neighbor as yourself?

(15) How does the scribe respond to Jesus' answer? What does this man reveal about himself in his response?

(16) Why does their questioning of Jesus stop here?

Mark 12:35-37

(17) What question does Jesus now ask? What wrong emphasis have the scribes apparently been giving in their teaching about the Christ? Notice what Bartimaeus called Jesus in Mark 10:47, 48. Note the people's acclaim in Mark 11:9, 10.

(18) What relationship between David and the Christ does Jesus want to make clear?

(Note—The people of Israel in Jesus' time held David in such high esteem because during his reign they had been free and victorious, and they expected that the Christ as Son of David would be a great political conqueror. Jesus does not deny that the Christ is the descendant of David, but he shows here that the concept of the Christ which the scribes were teaching was much too low, that the Christ is not only David's son but David's Lord. *Lord* is the regular translation of *Jehovah* in the Greek version of the Hebrew Scriptures.)

Mark 12:38-44

(19) What six things characterize the scribes against whom Jesus is giving a warning? What do all these things add up to? Which of these things must we be alert to avoid ourselves? Why is their condemnation to be greater? What opportunity and what responsibility do they as scribes have?

(20) How does the poor widow compare with the scribes and with the many rich people? What lesson does Jesus point out to his disciples? Compare her act with his words in verse 30.

SUMMARY

(1) How would you describe the various people who question Jesus in this chapter? How many times does Jesus quote Scripture in answering their questions? What does this show about Jesus' view of the Old Testament?

(2) What particular teachings does Jesus emphasize at this point? If you had been one of the twelve disciples what especially would you remember from this section?

CONCLUSION

The temple becomes Jesus' headquarters for teaching but since it is also the headquarters of those who wish to destroy him it becomes a place of challenge and conflict. Yet, even in this atmosphere there are individuals like the scribe in verses 28-34 who respond with spiritual insight.

Things to Come

The thinking throughout this chapter is in terms of Jewish history and Jewish ideas familiar to the Jews of Jesus' day but strange and therefore difficult to us. This chapter contains the prophetic teachings of Jesus and specifically the prophecy of two major events in history— the fall of Jerusalem and Jesus' own second coming. Both events were future to the time when Jesus spoke. The first event prophesied was fulfilled in 70 A.D., but Jesus' second coming is still future.

Mark 13:1-8

(1) When and where does this discussion take place? What initiates the conversation? What does Jesus say about the temple?

(Note—One of the wonders of the world of that day, the temple was built of huge stones, some of them forty feet long, twelve feet high, and eighteen feet wide. Little wonder that their size and splendor impressed the Galileans.)

(2) What do these four disciples want to know about Jesus' prophecy? Why? What would the destruction of the temple mean as far as the Jews were concerned?

(3) Instead of answering their question immediately, what warning does Jesus give them (verses 5, 6)? Why would this be more important? In what realm does the real danger lie?

(4) What types of things does Jesus describe will happen (verses 7, 8)? Who would be affected by these calamities? (To the people thus affected, these things would surely seem to indicate the end of the world, but Jesus says, "Do not be alarmed . . . the end is not yet, . . . this is but the beginning of sufferings.")

Mark 13:9-13

(5) In addition to the general calamities what specific troubles does Jesus foretell for his followers? From what groups will pressure come? Why? What job will the Christians have?

See Mark 1:1, 15 for previous references to the *gospel* in Mark. For whom is the message of the gospel intended?

(6) What command and what promise does Jesus give to those who bear testimony for him? Why would one be tempted to be anxious about what he is going to say?

(7) To what extent and from what unexpected quarter will persecution come? Why is this the hardest to bear? Observe the reason for persecution mentioned in verses 9 and 13. What response is called for under this persecution? What promise is given?

(8) From this paragraph how would you define the role of the church in the world?

Mark 13:14-23

(Note—When Jesus spoke of *the desolating sacrilege* or *the abomination of desolation,* his hearers would be reminded of the prophecy in Daniel 9:27; 11:31; 12:11 and also of the event which occurred about 170 B.C. when Antiochus Epiphanes, the king of Syria, captured Jerusalem, set up an altar to Zeus in the temple, sacrificed swine upon that altar, and turned the courts of the temple into public brothels. In mentioning the desolating sacrilege Jesus is warning that such a thing will happen again.)

(9) Compare verses 14-16 with Luke 21:20-22. In each case, what specific sign, warning and advice does Jesus give?

(10) Upon whom will the suddenness and severity of the situation bring special hardship (verses 18-20)? Why do women and children always suffer most in times of calamity? How does the Lord show his mercy? Why? (verse 20)

(Note—It is significant to note that the Christians of Jerusalem did heed the words of Jesus and departed from the city prior to its siege and subsequent fall in 70 A.D. They thereby escaped the siege and destruction in which 97,000 were taken captive and 1,100,000 died from hunger and the sword.)

(11) Against what danger other than physical danger does Jesus warn? What commands does he give in this connection? Why should we not be swayed by signs and wonders?

Compare verses 21-23 with verses 5, 6, 13. What is the real danger for the Christian through the years? What forms do false prophets and false Christs take today?

(12) How does Jesus say that his return (the coming

of the Son of man) will be clearly distinguishable from that of all false Christs and prophets? With Mark 13:21, 22 compare Matthew 24:23-27, noting especially verse 27.

Mark 13:24-27

(13) What things does Jesus describe as accompanying the second great crisis event? When will these events take place? Compare the first phrase of verse 14 with the first phrase of verse 26. How does the difference in pronoun indicate that the second event would be in a different age than the first?

(14) How will Jesus Christ come again? What will he do when he comes?

Mark 13:28-37

(15) What further teaching does Jesus give concerning the timing of events?

(Note—*All these things* in verse 30 is generally held to refer to the things foretold concerning the fall of Jerusalem which took place in 70 A.D. within the lifetime of those who heard Jesus speak.) How does verse 32 substantiate the thought that verse 30 does not refer to Jesus' second coming?

(16) Considering the prophecies of the chapter, what comfort does Jesus' promise (verse 31) give?

(17) In the light of verse 32, what commands does Jesus give? What does his illustration (verses 33-37) emphasize?

SUMMARY

(1) Describe the two major events foretold in this chapter.

(2) What are the major commands and warnings in this chapter?

(3) If you had been one of the disciples (verse 3) what especially would stick in your memory?

CONCLUSION

Those who disregarded Jesus' prophecy concerning the fall of Jerusalem did so to their own peril. There are those today who disregard his words concerning his coming again in power. But Jesus tells us that history is moving toward its end, and that he is involved in the course of history and its culmination.

DISCUSSION 15—MARK 14

Last Supper Betrayal and Trial

The final events before the crucifixion are related in detail in this chapter of high emotion and sharp contrasts. The reader will benefit from reading imaginatively and entering into each situation.

Mark 14:1-11

(1) Compare the attitudes toward Jesus held by the various people in this section. What attitude do those in verse 4 have toward Jesus and his worthiness?

(2) What evaluation does Jesus make of the incident (verses 3-9)? What decision does Judas now make?

Mark 14:12-25

(3) What preparations has Jesus made in order to celebrate the Passover with his disciples (verses 12-16)? Why might the mention of the exact address of the place be a danger at this point? What is Judas now seeking?

(4) What does Jesus reveal to his disciples as they are eating? What is their reaction, and what does their question reveal?

(5) What is Jesus seeking to impress upon his disciples in verses 22-25? What is a covenant? What does Jesus again foretell?

Mark 14:26-31

(6) What moves Peter to make his boast in verse 29? What is the implied insult to the other disciples?

(7) What does Jesus know about Peter that Peter does not yet know about himself?

(8) Why does Peter make his boast and pledge even stronger? What do the others do?

Mark 14:32-42

(9) What insight do you get into the heart and mind of Jesus? How do his disciples fail him? Why? How does he react? What do his questions indicate?

(10) What has made this hour supremely lonely for Jesus?

Mark 14:43-52

(11) Imagine yourself a film director assigned to re-produce the events recorded in this section. Describe your scenery, props, costumes, characters, and action. What major impressions do you want to make on those who will see the film?

(12) What type of group is sent to arrest Jesus? How does Jesus respond in the situation? To what is he submissive? How are the words of Jesus in verse 27 fulfilled? Why, do you think, have Peter and the others fled?

(13) Many believe that verses 51, 52 are Mark's own testimony and experience. It is probable that the Last Supper was eaten in the upper room of Mark's mother's house. The linen cloth was probably Mark's bed-sheet and he may have been on his way to warn Jesus against the mob which he heard approaching through the night.

Mark 14:53-65

(14) The Sanhedrin broke all its own laws in this trial of Jesus. Describe the scene. What problem does this supreme court of the Jews have? What is their goal? What specific accusations are mentioned?

(15) What indicates the frustration of the high priest in this situation? What position does he hold in Israel? What questions does he ask Jesus? Which question does Jesus not answer? Which does he answer? What claim does Jesus make?

(16) How does the high priest react to Jesus' claim? What do the others do? What becomes the main issue in the trial? How does Jesus himself make this the issue?

Mark 14:66-72

(17) How does verse 54 show that Peter is perhaps the bravest of the disciples? How is each of the accusations made to Peter a greater threat to him than the one before? What progress do you observe in the way in which Peter answers? Why doesn't Peter leave after the first accusation?

(18) What does verse 72 reveal about Peter? How are we sometimes like Peter disciples of courage, cowardice and remorse? Compare the pressures Peter faced with the pressures which Christians face today.

SUMMARY

(1) Describe Jesus as he appears in each of the situations in this chapter.

(2) What impressions do you get of Jesus' friends? of his enemies?

CONCLUSION

This is a chapter of tenderness and terror, intimate fellowship and stark loneliness, brave words and feeble deeds. The thoughtful reader cannot help but be aware of the profound emotion of these last hours before Jesus is parted from his disciples.

DISCUSSION 16—MARK 15

Before Pilate
Crucifixion

Jesus spoke many times to his disciples about his death. At least twice he spoke of the purpose of his death—"a ransom for many" and "my blood of the covenant, which is poured out for many" (Mark 10:45; 14:24). In this chapter his words are fulfilled.

Mark 15:1-15

(1) What problem now faces the council? What do they decide to do?

(2) What questions does Pilate ask Jesus? Which does Jesus answer and how? Compare with the questions asked him at the trial before the council and the answers he gave there. See Mark 14:60-62. What similarities do you observe?

(3) What does Pilate mean when he asks Jesus if he is king of the Jews? About what must Pilate wonder?

(4) What custom has been established which gives Pilate an opportunity to mollify the crowds? What do you learn about Barabbas?

(Note—The name Barabbas means "a son of a father" in contrast to Jesus who is "the Son of the Father.")

(5) How does Pilate hope to use this custom to his own advantage? How do you know that he is not blind to the true issues in the situation?

(6) How does Pilate try to avoid responsibility in the trial? What chain of command do you observe? Who runs Pilate and who runs the crowds? What is Pilate's motivation? What should be his motivation under Roman law?

(7) Read aloud Pilate's three questions in verses 9, 12, 14. What do they reveal about Pilate? What do the answers to these questions reveal about the chief priests and the crowd? What choices are they making?

Mark 15:16-32

(8) How are the words of Jesus in Mark 10:33, 34 fulfilled in verses 16-20? What has Jesus already suffered?

See verse 15. (Scourging in itself could be a death penalty, and few remained conscious through it.) Who takes part in the mockery?

(9) If, as is probable, Simon of Cyrene is coming to Jerusalem to celebrate the Passover, what does he have on his mind when he is compelled to carry the cross? Although he does not know it at the time, how is he finding what his heart is searching for?

(Note—Many scholars believe that Simon did become a Christian and that he is mentioned in Acts 13:1 and his family in Romans 16:13.)

(10) What specific details does Mark mention in connection with the crucifixion? What is the significance of the details mentioned? The offer in verse 23 was an act of mercy. Drugged wine would ease the pain. Why does Jesus refuse it?

(11) Compare verse 24 with Psalm 22:18, and verses 29-32 with Psalm 22:6-8.

(12) Why does Jesus not save himself as he is challenged to do? Remember his words in 10:45 and 14:24. What indicates the chief priests clearly understand the claim of Jesus that they are rejecting?

(13) Do you think that the chief priests would have believed if Jesus had come down from the cross? If not, why not?

Mark 15:33-41

(14) Compare the reactions to the crucifixion in verses 22-32 with the four statements reflecting the true meaning of the crucifixion in verses 33, 34, 38, 39. What does each of these statements tell us about what was happening as Jesus died?

(15) What is the significance of Jesus' cry? Why must he suffer this ultimate separation? How are Jesus' words misunderstood? What does the speculation of the people at a time like this reveal about them?

(16) What does the way in which the curtain of the temple is torn indicate? (This is the heavy curtain which stood before the Holy of Holies, and through this curtain the high priest entered once a year to make atonement for the sins of the people.) Why is the way now open to the presence of God?

(17) To what has this centurion been a witness (verse 16)? How do you account for his testimony?

(18) What other witnesses are there? Why are the women present but the disciples are not?

Mark 15:42-47

(19) Describe the scene between Pilate and Joseph as you see it in your imagination. What do you know about Joseph? What surprises Pilate?

(20) What specific things does Joseph do? Since the Sabbath began at sundown on Friday and work was then forbidden, there was urgency in Joseph's work. Who observes his service?

(21) Some scholars think that as a sympathizer with Jesus, Joseph may not have been summoned to the illegal night trial at the high priest's house. Nevertheless, there is a strong possibility that he was there and that at a later date he revealed the events of the night to the other disciples. If the latter idea is true, compare Joseph as one of those present in 14:53-65 with the Joseph we see in 15:42-46. How do you account for the change in him from a secret follower to a committed one? Do you know of any people today who have had a similar experience?

SUMMARY

(1) Comparing the two trials (14:53-65 with 15:1-5), how does Jesus make clear in each trial that the issue is his claim to be the Christ?

(2) Have each person in the group choose one of the characters or groups in this chapter and have him describe the events of the day to a friend (e.g. as a soldier saw it, or as Simon of Cyrene saw it).

CONCLUSION

"Therefore, brethren, since we have confidence to enter the sanctuary by the blood of Jesus, by the new and living way which he opened for us through the curtain, that is, through his flesh, and since we have a great priest over the house of God, let us draw near with a true heart in full assurance of faith, with our hearts sprinkled clean from an evil conscience and our bodies washed with pure water." (Hebrews 10:19-22)

DISCUSSION 17—MARK 16:1-8
LUKE 24

Resurrection

In all the great early manuscripts available to scholars the Gospel of Mark ends at 16:8. It is obvious, however, that the story is not over and the most plausible explanation is that the original ending of this account was lost. For a fuller view of the resurrection, study Luke 24 in conjunction with Mark 16.

Mark 16:1-8

(1) Picture the women as they approach the tomb. Who are they? Why are they going to the tomb? What problem do they foresee?

(2) What do they see in the tomb? What do they learn? Why should they not be amazed? What instructions are they given? Compare with 14:28. How do the women react?

Luke 24:1-35

(3) What details does Luke add in verses 1-12 to Mark's account of the women's experience? Why don't the apostles accept the women's story?

(4) Describe the two who are on their way to Emmaus. What are they thinking and talking about? How do they feel? Why are they so discouraged?

(5) Why does Jesus call them foolish and slow of heart to believe?

(6) Describe the Bible study Jesus has with these two people. Why does this study of the Old Testament Scriptures precede Jesus' revealing himself to them? Why do they need a Bible study?

(7) Why do they invite Jesus to stay with them? What does this show about these bereaved disciples?

(8) When and how do they recognize Jesus? What is their testimony? What do they do immediately? Why?

(9) What do they learn upon their return to Jerusalem? (Jerusalem is about 7 miles from Emmaus.)

Luke 24:36-53

(10) What is their reaction to Jesus' sudden appearance in their midst? Why? What does Jesus emphasize about himself? Of what are the disciples finally convinced? Contrast their feelings in verse 41 with their feelings in verse 17. What accounts for the difference?

(11) What effect would Jesus' eating have upon his disciples? Of what would this assure them?

(12) What does Jesus want his disciples to understand about the Old Testament Scriptures? What special advantage is given to them at this time? Why is it important for the disciples to understand the Scriptures?

(13) What message is to be preached? How and to whom? Compare the message here with that of John the Baptist (Mark 1:4) and Jesus' message at the beginning of his ministry (Mark 1:15). What is repentance? Why is repentance a prerequisite to forgiveness?

(14) What commission and instructions and promise does Jesus give to his disciples? Why will they need power from on high? How have the events immediately preceding the crucifixion revealed the lack of power among the disciples?

(15) What is the atmosphere of Jesus' departure described in verses 50-53? What do the disciples do when Jesus leaves them? What does their going to the temple indicate? Why are they unafraid now to go to the headquarters of those who put Jesus to death?

SUMMARY

(1) How is a bodily resurrection emphasized in this chapter? What difference did Jesus' resurrection make to his disciples? What practical difference does His resurrection make to you today?

(2) Why, do you think, do the study and the understanding of the Scriptures play such an important part in this chapter?

CONCLUSION

Many have called the resurrection God's seal of approval to all that Jesus said and claimed and did. The fact that the Lord Jesus Christ is risen from the dead becomes the major theme of the early church's message in the book of Acts.

Conclusion

At the beginning of his account Mark declared that Jesus was the Messiah (Christ), the Son of God. Chapter by chapter he has related Jesus' statements that he came to call sinners, to plant the seed of God's word, to serve men, to die and rise again. He has related Jesus' actions in casting out evil spirits, calming wind and waves, walking on the sea, multiplying bread and fish, forgiving sins, healing the sick, raising the dead.

Mark has devoted over one-third of his book to the details of Jesus' suffering and death because he wanted his readers to appreciate the significance of these shattering events as they fulfilled Jesus' statement that he came to give his life a ransom for many. Jesus called for commitment and discipleship and he still presents each man with a choice—to follow Jesus and let him rule in his life, or to follow the pursuits of this world and in the end forfeit his soul.

Jesus called people to follow him, and you have read of the men and women of his day who did that. You have examined the record, seen Jesus' life, death and resurrection. You have heard his teachings and his promises. What is *your* decision about Jesus Christ? Will you invite Him into your life? Will you ask Him to forgive your sins and become your Savior? Will you acknowledge Him as your Lord?

This page may be used for study notes.

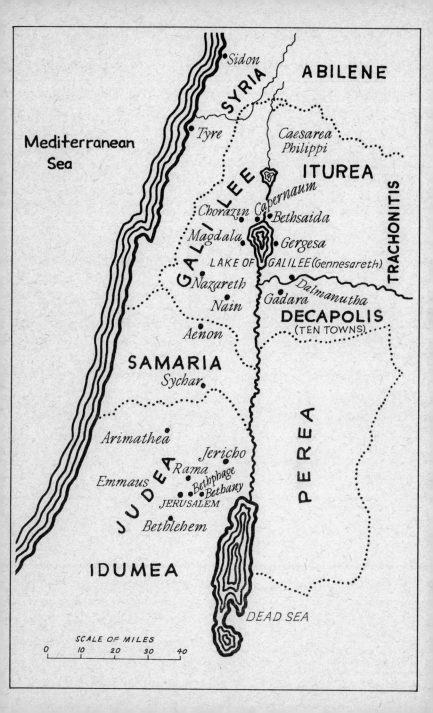